Wal

Other books available through
Stockport Publishing, LLC

The Rodeo Road, 2012

Eight Seconds of Grace, 2014

Walk Like A Man

By Bruce Ford

Thad Beery, Editor

Stockport Publishing, LLC

Stockport, Ohio, 2015

Cover Photo by Dave Jennings
Bruce Ford aboard Khadafy Skoal
Cheyenne Frontier Days, 1989

Design and Editing by Thad Beery

Library of Congress Control Number: 2015949994

ISBN: 978-0-9916482-1-4

DEDICATION

When I asked Bruce, "Who do you want to dedicate your book to?" he said—with no hesitation—"To you. I have a lot of loving family, but the book should be dedicated to you for putting it together."

Humbly, Thad Beery

CONTENTS

FOREWORD

I remember watching Bruce Ford ride before he won those five world bareback riding titles, before he became the first cowboy to win $100,000 in a single event in a year, and before he set or tied all the bareback riding records. He rode with the old flat-bodied riggin' they used back in the day, unlike the new-style, high-bodied, ramped up deal they use now. Yet, he rode that old riggin' in the style of today, laid way back on the bronc, looking so far up that you just knew all he could see was the sky—if he had his eyes open at all. He didn't wear a neck pad or flak jacket for protection. It's a testament to his athleticism and conditioning that a white roll of doctor tape was his only aid. He was so far ahead of his time—laying his spine right down against the backbone of the horse, spurring high and wild, ripping his feet clear to the rigging each jump and gapping his legs out wide—that they still ride that way today.

At that time a lot of the old hold-overs from the previous era were still riding in the controlled sit-up style, working their feet up and down the bronc's neck, but always keeping them in close to the horse. They were aghast looking upon this new *two-hundred-mile-per-hour* style. Some were critical of the nearly out-of-control rides Bruce was making. But along with the risk he took every time he "let 'er fly" came rewards. Big rewards. His career started hot and kept building momentum through 19 National Finals Rodeo qualifications.

When you'd see him and his brother, Glen—another world-class bareback rider—at a rodeo, you just watched and listened, and stood as close as you dared to get, hoping a little bit of that way they had of doing things would rub off on you. It was the grit and attitude that defined a whole era in the sport. Bruce, and those others he rode with, set a standard for future cowboys to emulate. Yet through all the wins, the awards and accolades, Bruce remained a friendly, outgoing person never in need of a bigger hat.

So, when I finished my first book of rodeo stories—the stories of my career—I sent it along to Bruce to get his opinion. He responded in kind, sending me his book, this book, and wondered if I could make anything of it. He thought maybe I could edit or even rewrite the stories for public consumption, and offered me free rein to do as I saw fit. After reading no more than a couple pages of his manuscript—written in a little chapbook in longhand—I realized I wasn't going to screw it up. Bruce writes in the same way he lives, bold and honest. His sincere voice comes through in his words and phrases like he is there beside you, telling you his stories, and that's the goal for any writer.

So my job as editor was simple. Run 'er through a spell checker, add punctuation here or there and leave the tone alone. The grammar may not be correct, but it is RIGHT. I hope you enjoy listening to one of the all-time greats tell it like it was as much as I did.

During the production of this book Bruce's home was hit by flood waters and destroyed. He told me how well he and the family were doing in the aftermath—friends rallied around them, people came out to help clean up and rebuild. He counted his blessings and felt lucky.

Then his foot got a sore on it and it put him in the hospital. It just wouldn't heal up. He said he'd been fighting diabetes most of his life—even during that incredible run of rodeo wins. They cut off part of his foot and he vowed that wasn't a part he needed anyway. He expressed thankfulness for his doctors and the great life he has.

Then they had to take his leg off at mid-thigh to quell an infection. Bruce was ecstatic with his prosthetic leg! It has an articulated knee joint that will allow him to get back on a saddle horse and ride when he gets it working right.

Always goal-oriented, Bruce is facing this most recent challenge with the tenacity he always displayed in the arena, praising the gifts he's been given and loving the challenge.

So go on Bruce, rip and charge, inspire us, and walk like a man.

Thad Beery, Editor
Stockport, Ohio, 2015

ACKNOWLEDGMENTS

I want to thank my family, especially my wife, Sherry, and my mom, Loretta, who are there every day. I appreciate the support my extended rodeo family has always given me. Thanks especially to all those appearing in this book. My life and career wouldn't have been possible without you.

FIRST FLIGHT

Sometimes events that happen out of the eyes of the rodeo fan would be greater ticket sellers than the actual entertainment we sell. I hope you will get some enjoyment from my lifetime of behind the scenes endeavors.

One of my first-time experiences came in the fall of 1971. My first airplane ride to Los Angeles, California, from Denver. My older brother by two and a half years, Glen, and I were on our way to the rodeo in Pomona, California. Glen was the big shot because he had rode in a plane before to go visit an aunt in Oregon.

We lit in Los Angeles, and Pomona looked to be right next to the L.A. airport according to our big map. Glen and I began walking, rigging bags over our shoulders, cowboy hats and all. We were approaching Century Boulevard when a bus driver offered us a ride. Knowing we would have to be good at saving money we passed on the ride, probably about a five dollar expense. About an hour later the same driver approached us again and asked where we were headed. We told him Pomona, and he said, "Pomona! It's forty miles across Los Angeles." So we broke down and bought a bus ride.

Upon arrival at the rodeo everyone was gone for the night. We would have been too bashful to inquire about anyone having a room, anyway. We had already spent money on the bus ride, so we needed to tighten up on sleeping arrangements. We found a concession stand—maybe the beer stand— made of a tarp. The desert gets mighty cold at night, so we wrapped up in the beer stand tarp and waited for that California sun to warm us up the next morning. We rode that afternoon and found that all the gold is not in California. We went home empty handed.

WALKAWAY PLAN

Travel seems to consist of a lot of my humorous experiences. I conduct several rodeo schools and sometimes have some students with some pretty good talent. One particular student we will refer to as "Robin." Robin had potential to be a pretty good hand and I invited him to go to some rodeos with me. This trip may have ruined him for life.

We started from Kersey, Colorado, en route to Vinita, Oklahoma. Now, I'm not a big believer in twenty to thirty thousand dollar rigs to rodeo in. My transportation I like to refer to as on the "Walkaway Plan," value $200 to $900, 1969 to maybe 1979 models, vans, Cadillacs, whatever starts.

On the Vinita trip, my 1974 Chevy hippy-type van began making a funny noise somewhere in Kansas. I told Robin to pull over. I checked the oil. It was good. Then I found a loose wire, pulled it off and it sounded a little better, but was running rough. After Vinita we were on our way to Mesquite, Texas, or Arkansas City, Kansas, Mesquite being our first choice. I've got an uncle just outside McAlester so we stayed there overnight. We did a tiny bit of backyard mechanics next morning, treated the van to new tires and were on our way to Mesquite. About fifteen miles down the road white

3

smoke blew from the engine and the old van spit the bit.

I got out and started taking junk out of the van. Robin said, "What are you doing?" I told him I was walking away from the van. He didn't believe me until I started taking the license plates off.

"You hitchhike south and I'll thumb north," I said. "Whoever gets a ride will determine if we go to Mesquite or Arkansas City. First car stopped and a man asked, "Aren't you Bruce Ford?" I told him we needed a different outfit and he took us to a wholesale lot where I bought another Walkaway van, a little nicer, $950, which got us to Arkansas City plus many more before I swapped it off.

The man still has my hippy-type van in Kiowa, Oklahoma. I've got a few scattered across the country but I don't have monthly payments due on any of them. That's the way the Walkaway Plan works.

FRIENDLY TRUCKER

I guess transportation has been a very humorous part of my rodeo career, but on this instance it became anything but funny. I had competed at the Houston Astrodome and it looked likely that I was going to qualify for the short go-round to be held on Sunday. I had promised my boy, Royce, that I would travel with him to Kearney, Nebraska, for a rodeo he was to compete in on Saturday. We left home early Saturday morning for a six-hour drive and arrived in Kearney that evening with a light snow beginning to fall. Knowing that I had to be in Houston the following day I should have left right then to go to Houston, but I wanted to watch Royce compete. After his ride (he won first, worth $800) I caught him a ride home and started out for Houston.

To my surprise, I-80 had been closed in both directions, east and west. I decided to call Houston and see just how good my position was there. The secretary said, "Good news, you won second in the second go-round, $3700, and are going into the short round in fourth position. Oh yes, I drawed a very good bucking horse, too. I decided to try and cut across country on the back roads. Let me tell you, when the interstate is closed the back roads get mighty deep with snow. After about ten miles of snow drifts, I decided to turn back. At about midnight I remembered highway 30 going east and found it to be pretty decent as far east as York, Nebraska. I then headed south on highway 81 toward Salina, Kansas, hoping to make Oklahoma City, for a morning flight to Houston where the rodeo was to begin at 3:40 P.M.

Well, 81 was slow traveling, about 20 miles per hour and still very little visibility. All I could see was the middle yellow line and I lost it about every ten seconds. About two in the morning I realized I was the only vehicle traveling the road. I also discovered I was going west when the road I was traveling was supposed to be going south. Then I dropped off in the ditch.

Snow blowing. Blizzard conditions. I knew I needed help right away. Me and the Lord had been having a conversation for quite a while and He was listening because I saw a farm house about a quarter of a mile back. I walked back to the house and began beating on the door. The dog started barking and a man in his Fruit-Of-the-Looms, with rifle in hand, hollered, "Who is it! What do you want?"

I said, "I'm a cold, wet cowboy and I'm coming in." He must have realized I was borderline crazy 'cause he put the gun down and let me in.

He and his wife put on their bib overalls and took me back to my car and pulled me out. For the rest of the morning the snowy road was pretty lonely. At about 4:30 A.M. I again got confused on my direction and run off the road just like before, only now I didn't see any farm house. I had a blanket in my car and figured I could wrap up in it until the sun came up and probably not freeze to death.

In about thirty minutes a truck pulled up beside me and I like to broke my neck hurrying to get out of my car. The poor guy probably thought he stopped for the town drunk or some weirdo. My shoulder sometimes comes out of joint, and when I went to open the truck door it popped out. I was squalin' and trying to get it back in. After it went in, I started to explain the situation with my arm. While reaching for his door it went out again. Finally, I explained I wasn't drunk but just had a bad shoulder and a stuck car and a rodeo to get to. He asked if I had anything to pull the car out with, and I said, "I sure do."

I opened my riggin' bag and pulled my bareback riggin' out and started cutting off my latigos. He said, "Just grab your stuff and get in. I'm going as far as Salina."

I said, "Not anymore. We're goin' to Wichita!"

We went pretty slow. He needed fuel at Salina, so I ran to the phone. I called my wife and asked her to call the secretary at Houston to tell her I was on my way and to hold my horse as long as they could. (You can only hold them to the end of your event.) Then I called the airline and got a flight that departed Wichita at 11:50, arriving in Houston at 3:25 with a stop in Memphis, Tennessee. With the rodeo starting at 3:40, even if I made the flight, I probably wouldn't make it from the airport to the Astrodome in time to ride.

I finally said, "Lord, you got me this far, why should I worry. It will all work out."

The truck driver rolled into the airport at about 11:35. I gave him a hundred dollar bill which he didn't want to take until I reminded him he probably saved my life. He then offered to go back the 140 miles and get my car.

I just made my plane and packed all of my gear on it with me. The guy at the gate scolded me and said the stewardess probably wouldn't let me pack it on the plane with me. I told him I was sure it would fit, and he said I could try. I put my riggin' under one seat, my boots under another and sat on my chaps.

When we landed in Memphis I began to get into my riding gear. I went to the rest room and put my riding pants on and my boots and spurs. When we took off from Memphis to Houston I went to the airplane restroom and attempted to tape my shoulder. I think I got more tape on the mirror than I did my shoulder.

We lit in Houston right on schedule and I ran for a taxi cab. I told the driver if he could have me at the Astrodome by four o'clock I'd give him an extra twenty bucks. "No problem," he says, and drove at about 70 or 80 miles an hour through traffic.

We arrive about 3:45 and I headed for the bucking chutes. The bareback riding was underway and one of my good pards, Larry Sandvick, grabbed my riggin' to put it on my horse. I told him about the latigo and he quickly fixed it—he knotted it up on the D-ring. I remembered I hadn't eaten since breakfast so I ran and grabbed a cookie and a pop. I'm a diabetic and could of got things out of whack pretty easy. Everyone kind of looked at me like I was a ghost because the story had grown from just running off in the ditch to being in a wreck with a truck involved.

My horse did a good job of bucking and I rode—considering all things—very relaxed. I won fourth and $7800. I called home to tell my family how I had done and my daughter, Courtney, said, "Yes! We know! We watched it on pay-per-view."

My family was relieved to see my face on the tube. I won't say that was all in a day's work, but things like that really build character. And like I said, I finally just said, "Handle it Lord," and prepared myself for opportunity.

GOTTA HAVE IT

You probably wonder where I come up with these Walkaway cars. I've done everything from paying cash, paying payments, to trading horses for them.

One year I convinced myself that I couldn't live without a convertible. I found a 1967 Ford in a residential area with a for sale sign on it. It was turquoise with a white rag top. Now they say love is blind and I must have been in love with this car because I thought it was beautiful and had to dig way down in my bag of tricks to convince my wife that I had to have this car. I told her my self-esteem would play an important part of having a good National Finals and that having this car would have a great impact on my self-esteem. As it turned out I did have a good National Finals and we cruised up and down the Las Vegas strip like cool folks of the 1960's.

But like a lot of things, when reality hit and snow fell in the great Colorado winters, I was ready for a trade. So one night when my family were all sound asleep I began looking through the *Fence Post* magazine, looking for a deal. The *Fence Post* is mostly an agriculture magazine and I was kind of horse shopping. Under "Horses For Sale Or Trade" I ran across an eye catcher. The ad read "Stretch Limousine For Sale." The price read "$7500 or trade for livestock." Being a man who swaps a few horses, I began to think I couldn't live without this Cadillac limousine. The car was in Rocky Ford, Colorado, about 200 miles from my home in Kersey. I called the man at about 10:30 P.M. and told him I didn't have $7500 but I shore had some stock. He said he would like some calves and I told him we could work something out. I was to compete in Houston that weekend and told him I'd be home on Monday morning. If he could have the car in my yard we would try to make a trade. I figured if he traveled 200 miles I would probably have the upper hand on the trade. As it turned out I didn't have any calves, he didn't need any horses, and he didn't want my convertible.

I bought the car for $2900, a pretty good whittle from the original $7500. The next day I set up a trade with my convertible with a car dealer who had three horses. I had to go to Loveland, about twenty miles away, for something. While at Loveland my car quit me. It was pouring rain and I called the car dealer who incidentally must have hated his horses. I told him the car had quit me. If he still wanted to trade three horses for a convertible bring your tow truck for me and the car.

We traded, and I later sold the horses for $3,000. Everybody gets lucky once in a while, but my theory held true. Always be prepared for opportunity. After a year or so of driving the limousine I realized the best seat was in the back watching TV. The lesson I learned from this is never trade for a limo unless you trade for a chauffeur in the deal.

BASS LAKE BLUES

My travel experiences haven't always been limited to cars. Small planes have been a very exciting part of my life. One year I was competing at a rodeo in Sulphur Springs, Texas. The next day I was scheduled to instruct a rodeo school at Bass Lake, Indiana, with Freckles Brown and Bobby Berger. I didn't really know how I was going to get there, but just knew there would be a way.

At Sulphur Springs I ran into Lyle Sankey, a great hand who absolutely loves teaching rodeo schools. He had a plane with a pilot chartered on a short term basis, so without too much arm twisting, and the fact that we would be working side by side with Freckles Brown, Lyle, the pilot, and myself were in the air for an all-night flight to Bass Lake.

I thought things were going pretty smooth, so I kicked back for a nap. What could go wrong in the spring of the year with no mountains within hundreds of miles?

At about 4:00 A.M. something started going wrong. I woke up and asked, "What's the problem?"

Lyle never has gotten real excited about things and was fresh out of college with a lot of practical jokes at arm's reach. He had that goofy grin on his face and said, "We're iced up!"

I said, "Turn on the deicer." But these were not jokes, this was a very serious conversation.

"No deicer here!" Lyle said, with a funny look on his face. I only found out later that Lyle knew another very good pilot who had flown him a few years before who had been killed in the same kind of situation.

This was in the spring of 1980 and I was to be married that fall. I thought about my wife to be reading about me being killed in a plane crash. I thought about my mom and dad reading the same thing. Then I doubled up my fist and hit the back of the seat. I realized that didn't do anything but make my hand sore.

The plane was at about 7,000 feet altitude and dropped to 3,000 feet in seconds. It was overcast and you didn't know when you were going to smash on the ground, but the saying you can taste death became a reality. I told Lyle we better get to praying. He said he had been. Pretty soon it sounded like a good church revival in that airplane. The wings were packed with ice. All of a sudden we broke out of the clouds into the clear and the ice started melting off the wings. We were lucky to make it to Bass Lake and land without a scratch.

We told our story to everyone at the school. I thought I would swear off planes for a while. When the school was over Lyle flew back with the pilot to return the plane. They ran out of gas en route and had to land prematurely. The Lord took care of us the first time. I'm just glad He blessed me with enough sense to avoid the second trip.

HEAVY PLANE

Another plane ride included Mickey Young and myself. We were competing during the Labor Day weekend rodeo run which sometimes is busier than the Fourth of July week. We had probably been to about seven rodeos in a three or four day time period and were making our last run of the week. We competed at Ellensburg, Washington, Friday afternoon and Walla Walla, Washington, that night. Saturday afternoon we were up at Evanston, Wyoming, and Winnemucca, Nevada, that night. Keep in mind Walla Walla is at about sea level and Evanston is about one mile above sea level. Something that's good to know if you're flying. The flight to Evanston went pretty smooth. In fact our pilot, world champion saddle bronc rider, Shawn Davis, even let Mickey fly from the copilot's seat some of the way.

It was very hot at Evanston and we were ready to head to a cool evening performance at Winnemucca after our rides. Shawn had taken care of all the details with the plane—flight clearance, filling the plane with gas and so forth. Mickey felt almost like a pilot now, since he had held on to the steering wheel for part of the flight to Evanston. Shawn had to settle up on the gas and told Mickey to taxi the plane up to where Shawn would be. Now I don't think this had anything to do with our adventure, but as I was sitting in the back seat I was sure hoping that plane didn't fly with us because I was sure Mickey didn't know any more than I did about planes. Which is nothing. He did a good job of taxiing the plane to where Shawn was waiting and I was ready to give him his little plastic wings. Shawn bragged on him and we headed for the runway with Shawn in control.

We got up some good ground speed and off we went. We were about as high off the ground as two telephone pole lengths when I heard this funny beeb-beeb-beeb. By this time we are about three miles from the airport.

"She ain't goin' to fly, boys!" Shawn said.

"Well, turn 'er around and let's land," I bellowed out like I thought you could do that.

We were experiencing what you call density altitude. Although the plane flew fine at sea level it just couldn't handle the same load and full tank of gas in hot weather at the high altitude.

"We can't turn. The plane will have to pick a place to crash."

It looked like we were going to be able to bounce it in on an alfalfa field, then trees, roads, and big ditches became a factor. We were about six feet off the ground and dropping when we came head on to a wire fence with about a twelve foot wide and twelve foot deep ditch on the other side. Shawn never panicked. He kind of wobbled the plane a little, and it just missed the wire and we were perfect landed on a gravel road. Shawn stopped the plane, looked around and said, "I guess we could use this road for a runway."

Mickey and I jumped out of the plane and kissed the ground. We taxied the plane back to the airport, trimming tree branches to drive on the road. Yet, miraculously, we didn't touch a branch when we were swerving in on this new-made runway. After the sun went down and we called to turn out at Winnemucca, we loaded up and took the plane back to Twin Falls, Idaho. I'm thankful Shawn and God were my pilots.

NASHVILLE TO KISSIMMEE

One year, I believe 1987, at the National Finals Rodeo, Monty Henson and a group from Tennessee were entertaining at the Fremont Hotel in Las Vegas. I had joined several jam sessions across the country and always considered myself a campfire cowboy singer. Monty invited me to get up and sing a few songs as I had done in the past for Larry Mahan, Chris LeDoux (before he got famous), and anyone else who needed a little break.

This Tennessee group just happened to have Gene Breeden, owner of a recording studio in Nashville, as lead guitar player. I do Hank Sr. pretty good and Gene invited me to Nashville to make a tape. I was to be in Nashville in mid-February, 1988. I really didn't know what songs I was going to put on the tape so I started practicing in the rodeo clown's dressing room in San Antonio, Texas, during the rodeo just days prior to my Nashville appointment. RC Patterson, a Colorado rancher and bareback rider had just bought a well-used van. He thought it would be fun to go to Nashville on his way to Kissimmee, Florida, where he and I were to compete in about three days. We ran into Bob Logue. He was up at Kissimmee the same as us and thought Nashville sounded like a good break from rodeo for a few days.

The trip down went smooth and to our surprise it was winter in Nashville, snow and cold. We went and found Gene Breeden and I reported for work. The musicians laid out a sound track to the songs I sung. Then some gals came in and what I call harmonized—they called it modulation.

Bob and RC decided to leave me working and go check out the sights of Nashville. They were excited to tell me of a place where Randy Travis was discovered—a honky tonk that was having an amateur night. So after a day at the office I was off to show my talents. I sang Kwalija because on a song that loud you don't have to sing good, just loud. But I did sound country 'cause I am country.

The next day I finally got to be in the glass room with ear phones on and sing my songs. Three thousand dollars later, and several tapes on their way to my house, we were off for an all-night drive to Kissimmee, Florida.

Somewhere just out of Macon, Georgia, a lot of smoke started coming out of RC's van. We coasted in to the only station within miles at one A.M. After a few cups of coffee and some serious transportation thoughts, we found a deal—a mechanic who lived in the country and had a 1965 something for sale, $600 or best offer. We called and told him our situation. We left the van to be fixed and negotiated for the car. Final price $400. What a deal! We were off again when all of a sudden, Bam! we were afoot again in the middle of nowhere.

It's about three A.M. We're as close to Atlanta as we are to our broke down van. We sat on the highway for some time before someone stopped. Bob and I heard RC talking to this guy and we started grabbing our junk to catch a ride. For some reason RC sent the guy on. He hadn't yet learned about the Walkaway Plan. We were leaving this 1965 something right where it sat.

After we sat for quite a while and began to get pretty chilly, we decided to pack all of our stuff to an overpass about a half mile up the road. We figured traffic would have to slow down enough to offer us a ride. Poor old RC had taken everything out of his van so he had a lot of gear to haul. We finally flagged down a truck driver and convinced him we could pack all of that stuff and three cowboys into his cab and sleeper and still leave him room to drive. He got us to the Atlanta airport in time to catch a flight to Orlando.

This story, like most of my disasters, has a happy ending. Bob won first, RC had a good trip, and I had a lot less money but a bunch of tapes with some music my dad and I had wrote and a lot of Hank's songs sung by me.

BIG L's BIG JOKE

You know, sometimes people get in a rut with their job, lifestyle, or just life in general. Cowboys are no different, I suppose. I have a good friend and top bull rider, Marty Staneart, who lives in Sanger, California, right near Clovis. At this particular time everyone was working the Clovis rodeo and a lot of cowboys stayed at Marty's mother, Jeanne's, house during this rodeo. Marty has two sisters and one younger brother, Philmore. Marty was going through a courting stage with his wife to be, so he wasn't hanging out with us this particular night. The sisters are both grown with one married and the other heavy into making a career. But all were home for the rodeo. It was just like home away from home. Nobody really wanted to hang out at Jim's Place, the local bar, so we were just kind of making things up to do as we went along.

We picked some strawberries from a nice farmer's patch. I guess he was nice, I never met him but he never shot at us either. After our strawberry feed, for some reason Philmore and a friend of his wanted to show us a pond about a mile from the house. Philmore and his friend were probably about ten or eleven years old, but they certainly knew how to help us pull off a trick.

Now as I get into this story remember, no one was drinking nor were they on drugs.

We just stopped the car and got out and started walking around. Bob Logue and I began to form a practical joke. We asked Philmore and his friend if they knew their way back home and they said, "No problem." They cut across country and were soon safe at home. Bob and me knowing they were home began hollering, "Philmore!" as loud as we could. The Hollywood really started coming out in us now! I looked at the pond (which was actually about six inches deep all over) and said, "I hate to think what I'm thinking."

Bobby said, "I'm thinking the same thing."

Lane Morris, a big bareback rider from east Texas was looking at us and saying, ". . . we got to find them boys." Somehow Bob and I had convinced Lane (whose nickname is Big L—that's what we all call him) that he was responsible for them boys, and Jeanne would kill him if anything happened. Fully dressed, I ran out into that pond and dropped to my stomach so Big L would think it was deep. Big L startled pulling his boots and shirt off, preparing to go on with the search.

I screamed, "No Big L! It's too deep!"

Bob said, "It's no use Big L. We've got to go tell his mom."

Big L couldn't believe something happened to those boys. How could he have let this happen? What was he going to tell Jeanne?

We convinced him we needed to go tell her. Once at the house Bob kept Big L outside long enough for me to fill Jeanne in on the joke. We also made sure Philmore stayed hid out. Big L came in, head bent way down, and told Jeanne the bad news.

Jeanne is the greatest actress I have ever seen. She was in tears. After her two daughters got her composure back for her, she went into action. She picked up the phone and pretended to call the police. We didn't know how long we could drag this out or what our next move would be, but Big L was really feeling miserable. And he hadn't even done anything wrong. But we never gave him time to figure that out.

Now, when you're on a roll, you can't mess up a good joke. Probably ten minutes after Jeanne called the police I pretended the police sirens were sounding and lights flashing all around the neighborhood. Big L thought we should go help, but we convinced him he would probably be held accountable for those boys so we better just let them handle it. You would have thought we were in a funeral home. We all knew it was a joke except Big L.

After about two hours we let Philmore appear with a story about how they were rescued. We decided to try and sleep but heard Big L telling Monk Dishman the whole story. Monk said we were just pulling a trick on him, but Big L refused to believe it. He said, "No, I seen the pond, the fire trucks. It was real!"

We pulled the joke and almost believed it ourselves. If this book is ever published everyone can come to my funeral because we swore never to tell Big L it wasn't true. To my knowledge he still thinks that all happened. Like I said—I kinda think it did—and I helped make it up.

COWBOY PRIVATE EYES

Clovis, California, always seems to have a story combined with the rodeo. In the spring, California seems to be a good place to rodeo. The only problem is if you live anywhere other than California it gets expensive to commute back and forth. Well, over the years a cowboy meets a lot of people that look forward to rolling out the welcome mat at the time of year when rodeos are in their area.

Clovis was a good place to locate because the rodeos were all Fridays, Saturdays, and Sundays. Being at Clovis was handy to get to Bakersfield, Oakdale, Red Bluff and others. A gal named Cathy put us up for about a month and we liked it there because she worked all day and had bicycles for us to ride to town or just ride around on. One time Mickey Young, Danny O'Haco and I spent some time there and got to know our way around pretty good. We knew where the western store was, the coffee shop and most everything else. Everybody began to know the three cowboys who were riding bikes around town every day.

Danny was the first guy I knew to own and rodeo in a Subaru station wagon. Later in life I made a commercial for Subaru and they gave me a car almost like Danny's. Good a car as I ever owned and the price was right. Anyway, Mickey and I had our rodeo equipment in the apartment, but Danny left his in the car. The next morning Danny went to his car to discover it had been broken into and all of his rodeo equipment had been stolen. Cathy quickly called the police and they suggested the robber probably went to San Francisco or Los Angeles to pawn all of the gear. Cathy decided to call the local western store and asked them to call us if anyone came in to sell the rodeo equipment.

We thought we were looking for a needle in a haystack as we didn't think anyone would be dumb enough to peddle stolen items in such a small town. But who ever said a thief was smart. Sure enough, about two hours after our call, the western store called and said there was a man there with a bareback riggin' for sale, and they knew we needed one—so come on down!

We jumped on our bicycles and headed for town. We decided Danny could hit this guy first, but we needed to get all of his gear before we scared him too bad.

When we got to the store this guy and his girlfriend were there with the bareback riggin'. Danny asked him where he got it. By this time the cops showed up.

Danny said, "You know whose riggin' this is?"

The guy said he got it about a year ago from old so and so.

Danny said, "That's *my* riggin'!"

The cops took the guy off and let us know they could handle the case. I think they were mad that we got to the store before they did. But we seen another mistake they were making, so we went into action. They took the man off but left the girl unattended by any police, so we jumped on our bikes and followed her. We sat and watched this big house she went into for about an hour. Pretty soon, police started arriving, probably about five cars. They looked at us, surprised, and said how did you know about this place.

We said, "Duh!"

It turned out they found all of Danny's equipment plus several bridles, saddles and tack. This turned out to be a warehouse for a crew of robbers. The cops didn't know if they should arrest us or make us honorary cops. At any rate, I'll bet there are still some folks in Clovis who remember the Cowboy Private Eyes.

MY GYPSY TRADE

Reading has always been one of my great enjoyments. I've learned to pass the time while traveling, or to relax prior to going to sleep with a good book. One of my favorite authors is Ben K. Green. His titles are *Horse Tradin'*, *More Horse Tradin'*, and *Village Horse Doctor*, to name a few. The reason I tell you this is because without one of his stories my next episode may not have taken place. The story was called, "Gypsy Hoss Trade."

One fall a man came by to buy a horse. He didn't have quite enough cash for the deal, but he did have a little 1983 Dodge Ram pickup. It had been modified a little as his boys needed an Ag project. It had a 318 Dodge engine which is pretty large for this little truck. The motor mounts looked like log chains holding the engine down.

I traded him a horse for $800 that I had given $600 for. The little truck ran good but would overheat every so often. During the time I had this little truck my indoor arena burned down. My tractor was also on the blink and my mom needed someone to haul debris away as she was foreman and main worker to get the arena mess cleaned up. That little truck served the purpose, and still took me to some rodeos.

I was on my way to a rodeo in Rock Springs, Wyoming, and went through Laramie on the way there. I saw some minivans on the car lots as I went through town. As I was traveling the little truck began to heat up. I would stop for a while to let it cool down, then off I'd go again. Each time it got hot I would think more and more of those vans. Finally, I made a decision. If that truck got hot one more time I was going to turn out at Rock Springs and go back to Laramie and trade for a van.

Sure enough, just outside of Rawlins it got hot. Good to my word, I turned around and headed for Laramie. I started talking to the man on the car lot and he said he was a Gypsy and his family had started in the car business after they had traded horses for several years. I thought we had something in common so I liked him right away. I traded him my truck and we agreed on $700 for a 1989 Dodge Caravan. So, I've got $100 in the van and am still driving it at the writing of this book— title and everything in order. A friend of mine who is involved in auto auctions asked me where I had gotten the van and I said, "Laramie." He asked if it was from the Gypsy. After I told him the story, he said, "You usually don't get your title . . ." and all of the usual pessimistic stuff.

About one year later, on my boy Royce's sixteenth birthday, we headed for Laramie. We found a 1991 Dodge Spirit car that needed the battery jumped so we could drive it. The Gypsies also had a 1986 Dodge Colt—a little wagon. They wanted $1500 for the Colt. I offered $1500 for the pair. After all the negotiating, I gave $900 for the Spirit.

"How much will you give for the Colt?" the old Gypsy asked.

"I don't want it," I said.

He kept shooting me a price as I walked for the door and I finally said $300. He hum-hawed around and then grabbed my $300 and gave me a title. He would have to send the title on the Spirit. We would have been on the road, but were trying our radios and other stuff out before we took off. Royce didn't have his license yet, so my nephew Jarrod would drive the Colt home. The Gypsy boy came out and said his dad needed to talk to me. Once inside, he asked if he could borrow $500. I told him I had gave all of my cash to his boys.

"How about you write me a check for $500 that I can give a guy today," he said, "and I'll write you one that will be good on Monday." He said his bank was not working with him very good. Actually, I thought he was just testing my loyalty. I said as long as his check was good.

"Oh, it's good. You have my word on it."

After about a week, he called and asked if the check had came back. I said, "No, and it better not!" About two weeks later, he said he mailed the title which never showed up. Then the check came back. As time went by, I decided to go to Laramie and put Ben K. Green's "Gypsy Hoss Trade" to work. I told Royce the plan and we were both excited, hoping we could pull it off.

We cased the car lot to see if there were any cars of value to cover our $900 car and our $500 check plus $100 for our trouble and a tank of gas. As soon as we pulled into the lot the old Gypsy pulled right in behind us. He was waving a paper and saying, "I've got your title!"

I looked at Royce and said we have got to stick to the plan. I said I would take the title—the kid was grounded, wrecked the car, but maybe I could sell it with the title. I gave him a picture and a cassette tape that I had made in Nashville. I told him we were looking for a nice car. We drove most of the cars on the lot and it was getting late, so I told Royce it was time for the kill. We had driven a 1991 Buick that would hold our money together. So we went and got in it. Our idea was to get a set of keys to start with. When we got in the car, here comes the Gypsy. Needing him to leave so I could get the keys, I asked about the car. He said he had $6,000 in it, but would take $4,700 just to sell it.

I said, "Would you take $4,000?"

He said, "Right now, today."

"Go get the papers ready," I told him. When he turned, I took the keys.

When we get inside the office, which was part of his house, everyone was listening to my tape. Then he asked who had the keys. I figured I was caught, but said I had them. He made his wife go clean the car out as she had been using it as the family car.

I've got my check book out, looking ready to write a check.

"We will have to send you the title!" he said.

"That will never do," I said.

The quick-thinking Gypsy said, "We've got a 1992 Chevy Blazer coming from Colorado Springs that will be here any minute, and we have the title right here."

"How much?" I asked.

The old man said, "$4,700." His boy blurted out, "But, we'll take a lot less!"

I told them I couldn't hardly buy a car I hadn't seen. Was it sure a good one?

"Oh, it's a good one. You have my word," the old man promised.

"If I have your word," I said, "I'll give $4,000 and you fill both rigs with gas."

"You want us to fill them with gas?" he asked. "How about $3950 and no gas?"

"Okay," I said, and he slid me a piece of paper which promised I was buying the car. I signed it, Ned Nuget, and handed it back.

He didn't look at the signature and just continued singing along with my tape. He stamped the title with my real name on it and gave me a temporary license. I still haven't put any ink to my check and started gathering up the papers. He took them back and said, "I'll give you an envelope."

"Naw, that's alright," I said, grabbing them up. I slipped my wallet back into my boot and they still hadn't realized they didn't have a check.

As I stood up, Royce tensed a little, thinking the fight was on. I said, "Boys, the ball's now in my court. That man owes me $500 for a bad check, plus $100 for trading with me."

He said he had talked to my wife about that, but I allowed he was dealing with me now. I told them Royce and I were going up the hill for coffee and would be back in thirty minutes. When we got back they could buy this $4,000 title for $600 or I would drive it home. I reached for the door and right then the Gypsy boys drove up with my Blazer. We smiled and said, "Good to see you!" and left, stopping for a second to get our keys out of our new Blazer.

When we returned, I had the title tucked in my shirt. I asked what they had come up with and the other boys got a little loud. I allowed that Royce and I had come to fight and the old man quickly calmed them down. Knowing we still had the title, the Gypsy said, "Here's what we've got, $400 in cash and we will send you $200 tomorrow. You have my word."

I said, "I had your word that you would send the title."

"I just gave that to you," he said.

I said, "I'll take the $400. You send me the $200. But everyone in this room stand up and testify, this is the best gougin' you ever took from a cowboy!"

"Oh, we didn't even see it comin'," he admitted.

We all shook hands and we left. My wife and mom weren't very impressed, saying we would never see the $200. A couple of days later it was in the mail box.

Me and the Gypsies have a good relationship now. But I'll need to be on my toes on our next trade.

WHAT'S KEPT ME GOING

It's hard to imagine that I have been as successful as I have with all these bad luck stories I've wrote about. But my life has really been a dream to anyone involved in the rodeo world. In fact the other day someone asked me a question that made me feel very fortunate and I was sincere with my answer. I am one of only a handful of cowboys that has won in excess of one million dollars. The question I was asked was, "Do you have any of the million dollars left." I thought for just a minute, and looked at the beautiful Rocky Mountains standing beyond my pasture. I looked at my fat tradin' horses, thought about my wife and kids, thought about my nice country home, and realized I still did what I wanted to do to make a living without punching in from 9 to 5. I said, "I guess I have it all."

But the money hasn't been my great success—it's the great people I've met. They didn't have to be world champions, but a person just bonds with certain people. After the achievements I've had it's fun to watch young people starting with their own success story. And after watching people like Marvin and Mark Garrett start from a young career to becoming multi-world champions it's even a greater thrill to see your own family begin their success trail. My daughter, Courtney, started at about eight years old. She had an old mare that was just a tad slow, but got her close enough to get bit by that competition bug. Later, we bought a young mare that Courtney began to train.

The first mare was Jenny. The next mare Courtney named Turn and Burn. She shortened that to TB. Anyway, she went on to win the world in the Little Britches Rodeo Association and also win the saddle for being the Colorado Junior Rodeo Association Champion. Pole Bending is her specialty, but she is also very good in the Barrel Race.

My boy, Royce, has been reserve champ in the Little Britches Association. Now sixteen years old, he was able to get his professional permit in Canada. He has done that, and him and I went to Calgary in the spring of 1998. We were both 78 points and got out of Canada with some money. Royce is doing well in the High School Rodeo Association. My wife has taken them to most of the rodeos and is their constant coach.

I've kind of just rambled in this chapter. I started to tell of my achievements, but I feel that you can read all of that in a ProRodeo Guide somewhere. I think it's important for me to mention the meaningful people in my life since this chapter is so off track. My friends that are more than just people I used to know are my best friend and brother Glen Ford, also, Rod Staudinger, John Clementi, Ike Sankey, Kenny Allinder, Stewart Sheldon, Bob and Chuck Logue, Marvin and Mark Garrett and Larry Sandvick. As I start my list I realize this book isn't big enough. If one of my pards—and there are many—aren't on this list, it don't mean nothing. I'm just writing them down as they pop into my head.

I'm very grateful for the bloodline I'm out of. I believe my dad was the greatest dad in the world, and my mom the greatest mom. They both taught me to seek Jesus as my Savior. Mom is a hard worker who still knows how to remind us Jesus is the answer. All I can say is thanks to my friends and family for giving me a greater goal. That goal is just being around good folks after my work is done in the arena.

TRAVELIN' PARDNERS

I'll start by telling you some of the things that happened while traveling with my brother Glen. Everyone has a different personality, but being a brother you have some of the same ideas. I think that's what draws you to any of the people you choose to be around. Glen has always been kind of a penny-pincher and he's always wanted to maintain control, especially if you are in his car and he's doing the driving. And he did do most of the driving because me or anyone who traveled with him knew how to use reverse psychology on him to get him to drive the whole way. Rod Staudinger and I would realize after traveling for several miles that it was about to become our turn to drive. Rod would begin to put a plan into action.

"I'll bet old Glen couldn't drive another 200 miles," he'd say.

"He could drive the whole way home!" I'd answer.

Rod and I would argue back and forth until I would finally say with a letdown in my voice that Rod was probably right. It didn't matter if we were in California with 1300 miles to go. Glen would be determined to show us that he could go that far with no problem. Rod and I would smile at each other and kick back for a nice long rest. Even when Glen figured out our deal he was so mad he drove anyway.

I mentioned him being a penny-pincher. That don't mean there's anything wrong with that, but I used to feel guilt from him if I ordered pie for dessert after a meal. And if you stopped for gas and bought a bag of chips or coffee or something, you would get scolded for wasting your money. To this day I don't think his family orders anything but water if they eat out. Another drawback when Glen was the captain, was the fact that you had better have a strong bladder, because when he was done pumping gas that car was leaving with or without you. And the thing about it is, you never knew when that was going to be. He could be using a pump where the price was 39.9 cents a gallon and see a sign up the road for 38.9 and just quit what he was doing to go up the road for cheaper gas. But he was the best I ever traveled with because my theory has always been that winners succeed by traveling with winners. And that was one of my first goals before I realized what goals were—I always wanted to ride as good as my big brother.

Probably my next best traveling pard was Ike Sankey. Ike was about three to four years younger than me, but impressed me and has impressed everyone else as having the knowledge of someone much older. And this thought started when he was 18 years old. Ike has red hair and inherited that ornery trait that goes along with most red heads. My first impression of Ike was that he was just a young-kid-flash-in-the-pan. But he wasn't cocky, he just portrayed that "I belong" attitude. "If you

like it, all right. If you don't, that's all right too."
He once had a horse called Moonshine—one of the
best of all time. He drawed this horse at Houston,
and most of the veterans had trouble riding him.
Ike didn't know Moonshine from the pony at
Walmart and made a great ride on him and won the
go-round.

Funny how being good at something makes
everyone your friend. But Ike didn't buy in to
superficial friendships. In fact we spent a lot of
time analyzing things. Like at the National Finals
people would come up and shake our hands, be glad
to see us and all that. We would look at each other
and comment on how that same person wouldn't
give us the time of day a month ago or a month
from now.

Every rodeo town has a honky tonk that's the
traditional place to get together. Fort Worth, Texas,
has several. But on Tuesdays there is a joint called
the Speak Easy that becomes cowboy night. It's
kind of a hippy hangout other than on this night.
Ike, myself, and another boy who didn't possess the
cool "so what" attitude that Ike and I had, flew to
Dallas/Fort Worth en route to Mineral Wells, Texas.
It's about a 60 mile trip from the airport to Mineral
Wells. Someone was supposed to pick us up and
take us to the rodeo. Ike and I sat down on our
riggin' bags and patiently waited as we watched
people go by, or maybe played cards for a while.
This boy is a nervous wreck knowing we had spent
money for the plane tickets, would have to pay our
entry fees and lose the opportunity to get on our
horses if our ride didn't hurry. I guess he thought

we would have a great solution to the problem if he just whined about it.

Finally, he looked at his watch and said, "We're not going to make it!" Remember, this is Tuesday night. Ike just looked at this boy in all seriousness and said, "Well, what are we gonna do? Go to the Speak Easy?" That probably don't seem humorous in this book, but after being there I still laugh at the statement. That's a reflection of how Ike approached everything in life.

Bob Logue and I could probably get to rodeos on a photo finish better than anyone. Bob is about eight years younger than me and probably added a few years to my rodeo career. I always said if a man could combine youthfulness with experience you would have it down. Well, I had won three world championships at this point and Bob was a young kid eager to do the same. Traveling all night and having only seconds to spare once you got to a rodeo were never a problem for us. The big problem was being at the rodeo town all day, waiting for the performance to begin that night. Because Bob's youthfulness included loving to play video games like *Frogger* or *Miss Pac Man*, which we later renamed "Miss Lil'" from the movie *Judge Roy Bean*, we would play these games right up until rodeo time and barely make it there to ride. Or we would have a night drive of maybe four hours but get hung up playing in some truck stop for about twelve hours.

He also had a nice little place in Cumby, Texas, that became our retreat from rodeo. He always had a couple of 3-wheelers that came to be called just 'wheelers. I'm not sure how the hippy communes worked, but this seemed a little like them. Bob's wife, Leslie, was an airline stewardess and was gone off and on. One time Bob, Mickey Young and I were all there. If Leslie wasn't on a flight, one or all of us were at a rodeo. One time we entered Bakersfield, California. Bob and Mickey didn't have good enough horses to lure them away from the 'wheelers. I had drawn a horse called Captain Jack—unfortunately good enough I couldn't stay home and ride the 'wheelers. I flew to Bakersfield and won the bareback riding. When I got back, Bob and Mickey reminded me of my kids when they were small. They both had that "Dad what did you get me?" look. For about a month it was that way, either Bob, Mickey, Leslie or myself were the bread winners. Mickey and I never paid a dime to stay there either. In fact, I don't think we ever paid for a can of gas to put in the 'wheelers.

One more comment on my buddy Ike. Him and I both rodeoed together in the early '70's. I've went on to win at the writing of this book five world championships. Ike chose to go into the stock contracting business. Last year he was chosen as the stock contractor of the year. I said earlier that winners run with winners. We are undoubtedly the names most mentioned when you talk about the greatest bareback rider or the greatest stock contractor. I appreciate the opportunity to have rodeoed with Ike Sankey.

SALT WATER BLUES

You meet a lot of people in the rodeo business. One of my long-lasting friendships came when I met Gary Moore. He was a few years older than I was, but had spent his begging years of rodeo in the amateur circuit. I had just took off in the Rodeo Cowboys Association and was fortunate to find success at a pretty fast pace. Gary had a riding style similar to Bob Mayo, a great bareback rider of the late '60's and early '70's. It was a style that stood out from the rest of the cowboys. Gary always came close, with a few minor problems such as missing his horse out, slapping his horse, or maybe a lower score than deserving. When he got an opportunity to win he really wanted to take advantage.

My brother, Glen, and Gary and myself entered a rodeo at Long Beach, California. It was about a 1200 mile trip from home so we had a lot of time to discuss how the judges had cheated us, or to brag about how good we were going to ride at Long Beach. Gary had drawn Cheyenne, probably the nicest horse in the entire world at that time, or probably even now. So, naturally, he got to proclaim all of the great things that were going to happen when we got there.

Well, Glen and I had about had all of the bragging we wanted to hear for one trip, so when

40

we got to Long Beach we set out to make our sorry trip worthwhile. The arena at Long Beach sits right on the beach next to the ocean. Cotton Rosser, the rodeo stock contractor, always tied his bucking horses to a picket line so the public could see how fat and well taken care of they were. Glen and I quickly went to the rodeo personnel to put our revenge plan into action. Everyone agreed to tell Gary that we had bad news. Cheyenne had gotten loose we told him, and drank the salt water from the ocean and died. The reride horse wasn't very good, but that's what he would have to get on.

Gary was so upset I thought he was going to cry. No, I'm pretty sure he did cry. Finally, we told him the truth. I think he was so mad he rode better. He went on to win second place at the rodeo. He finished behind Joe Alexander, who was the greatest bareback rider in the world at that time.

Gary retired after he won the Mountain States Circuit Finals Championship in 1979. He is now the President of Centennial Bank. But don't ever think the people you meet in rodeo can't help you. Because I have so many Long Beach stories to tell on Gary I get loans anytime I need them, no questions, no collateral. Thanks for your friendship and occasional slip-ups Gary.

VERNAL TRUCK RIDE

The "Vernal Truck Ride" story is actually a two-part story. It starts with an early morning airplane ride from Greeley, Colorado, to Prescott, Arizona.

Lonnie Hall, Bob Logue and myself, employed a local farm boy with a pilot's license to fly us to Prescott. For no particular reason I was in the copilot's seat. After about 50 miles in the air the radio began squawking that we were on an unannounced flight going over the Denver airport. We got lined out just in time to be told we were in an area over Colorado Springs that was restricted. Finally, we started heading across the mountains. Farm Boy decides we need to land at Alamosa, Colorado, for a new map. So far, Bob is envious of me being the copilot and sure wants his chance at the job.

After we landed at Alamosa without clearance we get a new map. Lonnie tries to find us a commercial flight but it can't be done so we get back in the plane. We are running short on time after our unneeded Alamosa stop, but Bob is the new copilot. He has to keep the plane level while Farm Boy looks at the map. Our ride gets pretty bumpy with Bob at the controls and Bob is getting pretty green.

Finally, Farm Boy says, "There's Prescott."

As we get close to the ground I see a water tower that says Crownpoint, New Mexico. Farm Boy hollers "Oh, no!" and about 45 minutes later we find Prescott. Planes are flying everywhere, and Farm boy dives right in like he knows what he's doing. Lonnie starts screaming at Farm Boy and he begins to panic. I said, "It's okay Farm Boy, they've got you on radar." The only radar he was on was probably a missile to blow us out of the sky.

Finally, we get on the ground and we're shaking. We borrowed a courtesy car from the airport and left Farm Boy there. We got to the rodeo just in time to ride and were relieved just to be alive. We were up that night at Vernal, Utah, and Lonnie and I would have cut them loose there, but Bob had a former bucking horse of the year so we figured we'd all die together.

When we got back to the airport Farm Boy was a different person. "Okay boys," he said, "Let's get her in the air."

We figured he did some studying 'cause this guy is different. He had serviced the plane while we were gone and seemed excited. We make a beautiful take off. We leaned our seats back in time to hear those wonderful words, "Oh, no!" again. Oil was all over the windshield. Farm Boy forgot to put on the oil cap. We got back on the ground. We quietly decided to charter a plane to Vernal. Farm Boy said, "Let's get a Cessna 210."

"Farm Boy," we said, "We're getting a 210, but we're getting a pilot with it—an' you're not him."

We finally get to Vernal. Bob got bucked off. Lonnie and I didn't want to go, but we split first and second at the rodeo. It's about ten o'clock at night and we're sitting in a restaurant wondering how we are going to get to Belle Fourche, South Dakota, the next day.

Bob and Lonnie were both married at the time. I was going with the girl that I married later that year. I was still free enough that I could talk to the opposite sex without being in trouble. There were a couple of girls in the restaurant. I told them our situation. This girl didn't know us from Adam, but I told her we needed her truck to go to South Dakota. We would be back in two days to ride at West Jordan, Utah. We made it to Belle Fourche alright. Bob and his wife got their van and followed me back to Vernal where we returned the truck. We got to West Jordan on time. We all laid back and watched fireworks after the rodeo and breathed a sigh of relief.

MOTEL ROOM SHUFFLE

I don't really know where this book will end. I haven't written in some time, but I read an article today in a rodeo magazine written by one of my former students and gained inspiration to write a story.

The student (I'll call him James) is young to the game of rodeo but is enjoying the tough-time-growing-pains of my early rodeo days. He and a couple of bareback riders from Colorado went on a rodeo run to Texas. The weather for the Texans was beautiful—but it was hot and humid if you were from Colorado. James had $50 total, the other boys probably less. But it was so hot they decided to spend $3.50 apiece for a ticket to a cool movie theater. After the movie they decided a bowling alley would allow comfort, so they sat and watched the bowlers and drunk water until the constant stares discouraged them. Then James remembered a story his instructor (me) told him. When the maids clean motel rooms they usually unlock several doors. So they slipped into one of the rooms and took quick showers. One of the cowboys being too clean for his own good, went to the front desk and asked for clean towels. They had to make a fast exit.

This brings me to my story. Marvin Garrett has been my student, my friend, and a great world

45

champion. However, this particular day Marv wanted to forget that he and I were friends. (I think he let being a world champ go to his head.) We had been competing at San Antonio, Texas, the biggest rodeo of the run we were on. It spans about a two week period. After competing in one of the earlier rounds we left for Tucson, Arizona. Then back across the country to Baton Rouge, Louisiana, stopping at some rodeos along the way. We left Baton Rouge after competing there and arrived back in San Antonio about four o'clock in the morning. Someone asked who was going to get the room. I remembered a key in my coat pocket from when we were there about a week and a half ago. I told them I had a room and they thought I was the hero. As soon as we got in the room everybody but me found a place to lay down. I jumped in the shower, brushed my teeth, got dressed and started waking up cowboys for their turn in the shower. They all thought I was pretty clever. When we got to the champ he thought we were playing a trick on him by telling him this was not our room. When he realized it was no joke he got pretty upset at ole 5-timer.

He said, "I thought you said you rented a room!"

I said, "I did, but it was about two weeks ago."

I didn't see the harm. We all had a good laugh, got clean and got the money at San Antonio.

The three stories that follow were told to me by Bruce. They are stories that he wanted to include in his book but he never found the time to write. We put them down here at the end of the book because it wouldn't be complete without them.

T.B.

SOMETHIN' SMELLS FISHY

By Thad Beery, as told by Bruce Ford

Fishy. Like when nine different eye-witnesses to a set of circumstances swear to nine different versions of the event.

Fishy. Like officers of the law making an arrest for disorderly conduct—citing public intoxication as a contributing factor—yet refusing to administer a breathalyzer test.

Fishy. Like the smell of some unrecognizable "mystery meat" hidden beneath slathered globs of thick gelatinous gravy served up by a temporarily under-employed future rock star biding her time waiting tables at an out-of-the-way truck stop until being discovered by a big record company's talent scout.

Fishy. Yet, all will be explained—perhaps to no one's satisfaction—shortly. Suffice it to say that nine witnesses rarely agree, officers of the law frequently say, "No comment!" when questioned,

47

and mystery meat by its very definition is fishy. So this author chose to write an "unofficial" version of the story rather than sort it all out.

The story actually begins with the incontrovertible and undeniable fact that Bruce and eight of his compadres had just won a major chunk of the prize money awarded at the Houston rodeo and being in high spirits in the afterglow of their wins were looking for a place to celebrate. Now, depending upon which members of the group you talk to, and which ones you believe, they were all somewhere between "stone cold sober—never had a drink in their life" and "three sheets to the wind" inebriated. So, they did what any discerning group of cowboys in a strange city far from home and familiar surroundings would do: They picked the first place they came across to party. In this instance that would be Boll Weevil's Truck Stop, Restaurant and Gift Emporium out on highway 9 between Hither and Yon. So, through the door of Mr. Weevil's establishment strutted eight happy and hungry cowboys, pockets flush with money, looking for something to eat. The ninth member of their posse remained in the parking lot to catch up on his sleep in the back of the van, suffering mightily from a lack of rest—or an excess of celebration.

They were greeted inside by linoleum topped tables, salt and pepper shakers, napkin holders and the empty stares of a couple dozen or so patrons who were suspicious of cowboys in general. After more than a few minutes—while they washed up, tucked in their shirts, pulled two tables together making one big table where they all could sit, and saw their conversation lag as their bellies growled over the menu—the cowboys looked around for their waitress who had evidently gone AWOL.

Bruce noticed a teenage girl behind the breakfast counter shuffling coffee cups around as she bee-bopped to some unheard music coming through her head phones while she lip-synched the words and smacked on a great gob of bubble gum. He tried to get her attention but she refused to see him waving his hand—even when their eyes met.

"Maybe she doesn't like you, Bruce," one cowboy kidded.

"I'll go get her," volunteered another, getting up from the table and heading in her direction. But she saw him coming and ducked through the double swinging doors into the kitchen in the nick of time. With no other waitresses in sight, the fella tucked in behind the breakfast counter next to the doors she'd escaped through, lying in wait. The whole table full of cowboys were watching by this time, so that when the bubble-gummer peeked out the little window in the doors to make sure the coast was clear, they all saw her.

"She don't like cowboys, period!" somebody said.

Seeing them all sitting patiently at their table, she braved a re-entry back into the restaurant. She pushed through the swinging doors, hung a quick left, avoided looking in their direction and ran right into the fella waiting behind the door who'd set the trap for her.

The whole table broke into laughter at the sight.

You could read the lips of the fella asking for service and pointing at their table. And you could read her lips as well, as she rolled her eyes up in that teenage way and with sagging shoulders mouthed, "Ohhh . . . OKAAAY!"

She had to find her order pad and slouched around behind the counter a minute or two getting ready to do some work. Finally, she removed her ear phones, laid the device behind the counter and wandered aimlessly in their direction talking—or lip-synching—to herself.

"Long time, no see!" one of the fellas greeted her when she finally got over to their table. You'd have sworn she never heard it, or the laughter that followed.

"Gimme a glass of water!" said the first guy to order, tossing his menu down on the table like that was all he wanted. Everybody laughed again.

Bruce noticed a couple of heavy-set middle aged guys frowning at him and his pardners from the next table. A couple of "Dough Boys," with spare tires around their middles. He smiled at them and nodded, which made them look away.

Somehow the waitress managed to take all their orders without speaking a word and never once looking up from her pad. When she turned the orders in at the pass-thru window to the kitchen she said a few words to a woman, evidently the cook, who shot a frown in their direction.

"Uh, oh," somebody said. "She told on us." Which led to more laughter. Which brought on another dirty look from the kitchen, the waitress, and the two Dough Boys at the next table.

The cowboys waited a long time for their meal, which was understandable with such a large order. In spite of their hunger it was becoming worth the wait as the atmosphere lifted. They got more creative in their humor. They were cracking jokes about the situation, the waitress—who had put on her earphones and fallen back into MTV mode, dancing and lip-synching behind her counter—and what kind of surprises the cook was planting in their dinners, unobserved.

After a while the waitress, without headphones, brought their drinks, still not looking directly at them. When one of the boys said, "Miss, I ordered an iced tea, not a Coke," she snapped, "You did not!" and gave him a look that would freeze flame.

Returning to her safe haven behind the breakfast counter, she jammed the headphones back on her head to demonstrate her disgust with cowboys and further insulate herself from any possible human interaction. This led one of the boys to refer to her as, "See no evil—Hear no evil," which, of course, she missed. But it led to more laughter, more dirty looks from the Dough Boys and the cook, who seemed to be keeping an eye on them, peeking out through the pass-thru from her kitchen at regular intervals.

By the time their meals finally arrived, Bruce was not surprised to find his was cold. Cold gravy slathered over some kind of funny-smelling mystery meat—and this is where we started this story.

"Somethin' smells fishy!" Bruce said to the waitress, pointing at the glop on his plate. "I'm not eatin' that!"

Everybody stopped what they were doing and looked at the waitress.

"Whaddya mean?" she whined, snapping a bubblegum bubble at the same time.

"It smells bad," Bruce reiterated. "I can't eat it."

"Let me seeee . . ." she said with a big 'Geeze!' shake of her head.

She stomped over by Bruce and with a condescending look, put her nose to his plate. Athlete that he was, endowed with lightning reflexes and impeccable timing, Bruce was able to not only stick the plate full of gooey gelatinous stuff into her face, but was able to actually twist it around and rub it in deep to all her senses. She came up sputtering, choking. She couldn't even open her eyes.

"Mom!" she wailed. "MOTHERRRR!" And out of the kitchen door burst the cook, like a mama bear defending her cub.

Chaos ensued: Miss MTV wailed; eight cowboys howled with laughter; Mama Bear—in full charge—roared at Bruce; and the Dough Boys from the next table jumped up and surrounded them all, producing badges like undercover restaurant critics. They were off-duty police officers who called a paddy wagon and arrested the whole cowboy contingent.

"All we did was tolerate bad service," one cowboy pointed out. To no avail.

They all went to jail where they tried to argue their case.

"We didn't do nothin'. Bruce was just playing a joke!"

Nobody was listening. The cop who processed them into the jail said they were charged with Drunk and Disorderly.

"We weren't even drinking," they claimed.

"The officers that witnessed the event will swear to it," the cop told them.

"The Dough Boys? They don't know if we were drinking or not!"

The booking officer didn't care, didn't even listen.

"We want a breathalyzer test!" they demanded. They got the drunk tank instead.

They were herded into a large cell—as cells go—where they lined up on a hard bench, sitting with their heads down in their hands. The stale air smelled bad. The government green paint was cracked and peeling. There were stains on the walls and floor from what you don't want to know. Add six inches of straw and it'd make a fine cage for animals. They each quietly contemplated their fate, their impending fine and their freedom, until somebody started to laugh. It was infectious.

"You really know how to rub it in, Bruce!"

"I saw it coming, but I couldn't believe you were actually gonna do it!"

"Did you hear her squeal . . . ?"

"And Mama Bear roar . . . ?"

It was the most heart-felt laughter the old dingy jail had ever seen.

"All in all . . ." Bruce said, grinning from ear to ear, "It was worth it."

Was that the consensus of the group as a whole? We'll never know because this story is fiction . . . and we didn't ask.

Epilogue

What of the ninth member of the group? The one that—according to who you ask—was either too drunk or too tired to go in the restaurant with the rest of the bunch and remained behind in the van catching up on his sleep. He'd won enough money to bail them all out of the pokey. Yet he didn't do it. Maybe he didn't condone their actions. Maybe he didn't think they were worth it. Or maybe he slept through the whole episode.

YER A COWBOY!

By Thad Beery, as told by Bruce Ford

So you wanna be a cowboy? You wanna find immediate fame and fortune on the back of a wild and mad, pitching buckin' horse? Bruce can help you out. Ask Bill Engvall who in one day—in fact in one minute—became a Bareback-Bronc-Ridin'-Rough-Stock-Cowboy! At forty years young.

You've probably heard of Bill, the stand-up comedian turned TV actor, country music performer, and game show host. You'd recognize Bill if you've ever seen the Jeff Foxworthy show on NBC where he was cast alongside Foxworthy, Ron White, and Larry the Cable Guy. He's the cowboy! And this is how it came about.

One day Bill decided to become a bareback rider—as Bruce would say, the first step toward doing anything is making up your mind to do it. So Bill showed up at Bruce's rodeo school. Bruce scrounged up a pair of chaps and spurs for him, found Bill a bareback riggin' to use, and ran the perfect bronc into the chute—a good old trustworthy "trainer" horse not much bigger than a Welsh pony.

When Bruce got the rig pulled down on the bronc, and Bill was all geared up in his cowboy duds, Bruce said, "You look good there, Cowboy!"

"I feel good," Bill replied.

"Do you feel Cowboy strong?" Bruce asked.

"I feel strong!" Bill answered.

"Well, climb up on this chute and put it on this ol' bronc, then!"

"I'm ready!" Bill hollered as he crammed his hand in the riggin'.

"Call for him 'outside' when yer ready there, Pard," Bruce encouraged.

"Outside!" Bill hollered and commenced to spur the bronc in the neck as a cowboy led the haltered horse out into the arena on the end of a lead rope.

"Are you okay, Cowboy!" Bruce yelled to the spurring dervish as the bronc ambled along.

"I'm okay!" Bill yelled back.

"Are you ready to ride!" Bruce hollered.

"I'm ready!"

Then Bruce turned to his trusty old dog and barked, "Git 'im Hank!"

When Hank nipped the heels of that bronc the horse kicked "Over his head!" according to Bruce. Bill took a long flight on a high arc, landing flat out in the dirt. When Bruce got to his side he had the wind knocked out of him and was laying in the arena gasping for breath.

"You alright, Bill?" Bruce asked.

Still struggling for enough wind to speak, Bill croaked, "That . . . that's the first time you've called me Bill."

And what of the fame and fortune that was promised at the beginning of this story? Well, Bill wrote a song about his experience—a country and western hit song. The music video is a highlight on his gold record album *Dorkfish* released by Warner Brothers Records in 1998. In the song Bill confidently and unabashedly proclaims, "I'm a cowboy!" Deservedly so.

FORTY SIX AIN'T OLD

By Thad Beery, as told by Bruce Ford

In 1992 Bruce hung up the riggin'. He had accomplished about all you can in the sport and was pushing forty years old. He'd qualified for eighteen National Finals Rodeos in a row, won five world bareback riding titles and one PRCA crown that would've been a sixth world title except for the unique way the association chose to name the world champions in 1978—the world champions from the years 1976-1978 were the NFR winners not the yearlong money leader as in all other years. He was still feeling good and riding good. He had a few other things he wanted to do, but what really made up his mind to retire was when he was at a rodeo with his son Royce and the announcer introduced him as "The son of five-time world champion Bruce Ford."

"I didn't want him carrying that load for the rest of his life," Bruce said. "I wanted him to make his own way." So he hung it up.

Things worked out fine. Bruce stayed closer to home and traded horses and Royce made his own way in the rodeo world qualifying for the NFR on numerous occasions and going on to become the 90th cowboy in rodeo history to post a million dollars in career earnings. Of course the rodeo bug hadn't left Bruce's system altogether (he still had a pulse) so that after a six-year retirement when a former student, traveling partner and fellow world champion bareback rider, Marvin Garrett, said to Bruce one day mostly in jest, "So, when are you cracking out again?" Bruce answered, "Right now!" Marvin gave him a kind of a funny look at that and down the road they went, just like old times.

And just like old times Bruce had a good year. He won $7800 at Houston, won a big check at Phoenix, won it all at Odessa and was off to a hot start. As the year was drawing to a close, he was ranked fourteenth in the world and set to qualify for his nineteenth NFR when he entered the Cow Palace Rodeo in San Francisco, the last regular season rodeo where the money won would go toward that year's NFR qualification.

At the Cow Palace, hanging out, Bruce was excited to be getting on and excited about the prospect of going to another NFR at the age of forty six. He was waiting for his pards Marvin and Mark Garrett to arrive so they could hook up and get a room. They were flying down from South Dakota in a borrowed airplane with a hired pilot that they regularly used.

Bruce waited and waited. They were long overdue. Then word circulated through the rodeo crowd that their plane had crashed, disastrously, forty miles short of the airport. A leaky fuel line had caused the plane to run out of gas. The pilot—a good friend—was killed, and Marvin and Mark were seriously injured along with a couple of other cowboys who were riding along.

Bruce went to the finals that year without his longtime friends. He had a good finals and finished the year in fifteenth place with over $50,000 won. It was the prevailing opinion of those who saw Bruce ride that year that "Forty six ain't old."

The following story was told to me by Bruce and his wife Sherry. For reasons that will become obvious Bruce was out of it about half the time and Sherry was his advocate, manager and secretary as well as his memory.

T. B.

THE TOUGHEST BRONC I EVER RODE

By Thad Beery, as told by Bruce and Sherry Ford

It would be easy to be a champion when you're on top of your game, riding well, with people everywhere recognizing your face and your name, and the money rolling in. It would be a lot harder when you're injured, suffering a run of bad luck, or over the hill with old age.

But I'd better back up and point out that there are two types of champions: Those that are crowned champion by virtue of winning a competition of some kind, and those that have an indomitable spirit that cannot be beaten whether they've ever won anything or not.

The first kind of champion is easy to pick out. You see them standing atop the Olympic podium receiving a gold medal, hoisting the Superbowl trophy for a parade lap around the stadium, or wearing a big gold buckle the size of a serving platter at the NFR. Everybody knows them. They get all the publicity. They're famous and usually rich. Their success is invariably accompanied by a big broad smile. Winning looks so easy when they do it.

But you often hear stories about this type of champion struggling when the cheering stops. They've put so much time and effort into their career that it consumes them at some point. It can take over their soul. When they are forced to quit competing—and usually they are *forced* to retire due to injury or age—they find it hard to replace the excitement of the career they've had. As Michael Strahan the ex-New York Giants defensive lineman and Super Bowl champion said in a 2015 interview for *Men's Journal*, "There's nothing you can do to match it. . . . The sooner you realize it, the better you'll be for it. There's nothing in life you can do. You can go jump out of planes all you want. You're not going to replace it."

The second type of champion—the one with the indomitable spirit—is harder to spot if they've never won anything big. This class of champion you have to get to know to appreciate. Their qualities may not be hailed in the arena or lauded in print. You'll most likely recognize them by the gracious way they take a loss or subtly keep coming back for more. They are much more adaptable post-retirement. They are proud of their career but it never defined them. They are able to move on.

The greatest champions—those that transcend their sport and influence legions of their followers long after their career is over—belong to both camps. They are the ones with the indomitable spirit who also happened to win the trophy. They tend to keep their athletic accomplishments in perspective, shelved into the bookcase of a larger life. These are self-motivated people. They don't need the roar of a crowd or the promise of a big payoff to perform. They attack everything they do with vigor and accept the results with a positive attitude. They are the true champions—champions at life.

Bruce Ford is one of these.

Back in 1997 Bruce's barn burned down. He lost a lot of tools and equipment as well as the structure, but reacted quickly to the emergency and praised the fact that they were able to save all the livestock.

Then in 2013 in an unprecedented occurrence the South Platte River reached unfathomable heights, leaving its banks a quarter mile behind to devastate Bruce's home. His response was to commiserate with neighbors in the area who'd suffered losses and pray for the best for ". . . all those others downriver." In the aftermath he praised his mother, Loretta, who took them in, and all the folks who wrote, called or came by with encouragement, some of whom offered support: labor, material, and even money.

While working to clean up the clutter and debris, Bruce stepped on a nail. The wound to a toe on his right foot got infected. Having battled the ravages of diabetes for most of his life—even back during his rodeo career—made the infection more dangerous than it otherwise would have been.

"I have sugar diabetes," Bruce explains. "Which was tough my last couple of years rodeoing. I went to the national finals with it." He adds that, "I've been on the rankest horses on the face of this earth, Sippin' Velvet, Mr. Smith, Three Bars. But the last episode in my life has been tough. I call it the 'Toughest Bronc I Ever Rode.'"

The toe landed Bruce in the hospital. When it refused to respond to treatment—the infection growing—the toe was amputated in the fall of 2013. Bruce's response was to praise his doctors for their skill and wave goodbye to a toe he, ". . . had no more use for anyway."

Back home and working on the house, with his balance compromised by the missing toe, Bruce fell one day and landed on his left knee. It hurt so bad he couldn't stand it. Everybody including his doctor told him that he had to get up and walk on that knee, but he couldn't. The pain was unbearable. Then one day, shortly thereafter, Bruce was at home and began babbling incoherently. His wife Sherry laid down the law.

"You're going to the emergency room!" she proclaimed. Since Bruce couldn't walk, a friend hoisted him on his back and carried him to the car.

"My blood sugar went to 1,800," Bruce says. "They took me to the hospital and laid me on a table and I literally died. My heart quit beating and they shocked me and brought me back to life." He jokes about it today, "I don't know if I went to hell or I went to heaven, but I don't remember any of it."

Bruce was diagnosed with a staph infection in the knee that had spread to his right arm and left shoulder. In all, Bruce endured three surgeries on his left knee, four or five—he lost count—on his right arm, and three surgeries on his left shoulder. An example of the gravity of the fight was when the doctors opened up his left shoulder and the infection oozed out.

He then went to a care home for further treatment and rehabilitation. His knee still hurt and the doctors didn't like the way the arm looked either. So in August of 2014 Bruce went back to the hospital for an MRI that revealed a lot of dead bone in the knee. A team of surgeons held a conference to decide on a course of action. The next day their verdict was explained to Bruce in no uncertain terms.

"You'll lose your leg or you'll lose your life," his doctor told him. The leg that spurred all those broncs, the leg that won all those awards, the leg that carried him for every step of his life would have to be removed.

"Well take 'er off then," Bruce said without hesitation. "I've got a lot to live for!"

The leg was removed at mid-thigh. He only spent about ten days in the hospital that time. They transferred him to a nursing home and he was fitted with a prosthetic leg. Sherry says, "There wasn't any, 'Boo Hoo, poor me . . .' in Bruce." He reacted like a champion—the type that takes a loss and keeps coming back for more.

But the nursing home was hard.

Bruce says, "Them nursing homes is for old people or people that's in bad trouble. It was more like a nut house than a nursing home . . . but I was there and away from my family. . . . It was pretty tough trying to learn to walk with that prosthetic leg.

"My wife'd come by with a couple old trading horses we had and everybody thought that was great that I could go out to the trailer and see my horses and look at my horses and different things, and we'd slip out and trade one off in the daytime and then I'd have to go back to the nursing home. And that was just driving me crazy. . . . But I'm lucky I've got a very smart wife who keeps us going trading a horse here and there.

"It was terrible . . . the loneliness you have in them deals . . . and all I did is, I'd sing some songs and everybody'd come around my room and they'd sing with me. And they'd try to teach me to walk about three hours every day. I'd try to get up and walk on this leg. And it's still been a battle. I've walked in a walker, I've walked with crutches . . . and, finally, I got two canes that's workin' pretty good for me . . . and I've got one a them little carts you get around in. . . .

"The thing about that is, I never lost my faith in the Lord, and I knew He'd get me through this deal. So I'm just amazed how things are working for me. . . . I need to count my blessings."

It became kind of a joke around the Ford place that at least once a day Bruce would fall. He couldn't feel the foot on the prosthetic leg and find his balance. For a while he had more bruises from bucking off that fake leg than he ever had during his rodeo days.

Sherry posted pictures on Facebook of Bruce using his new prosthetic leg in rehab. He praised the articulated limb, saying, "It's computerized. The doctors tell me I'll be able to grip with it once I get it goin'. I'll be able to ride again!"

He set a goal to ride a horse by December. And sure enough on Christmas Eve he did— bareback of course.

ABOUT THE AUTHOR

Bruce Ford lives on the home place near Kersey, Colorado, with his wife, Sherry, and mother, Loretta. They are rebuilding after a flood's devastation. He was recovering his health as this book was coming together and, as always, Bruce "Trades a few horses. . . ."

Made in the USA
San Bernardino, CA
29 June 2018